blodyn

by

Derec Jones

Published by:

**OPENING
CHAPTER**

First Printing, 2017

ISBN 10: 1-904958-62-1

ISBN 13: 978-1-904958-62-8

published by:

Opening Chapter
Cardiff, Wales

openingchapter.com

To all you little flowers

more at derecjones.com

INTRODUCTION
February 2017

The poems in this collection have been selected from work that spans more than half a century. They are in no particular order but have been chosen to represent as many styles and to present as much variety of content as possible.

A few of the poems have been published before.

About Blodyn
This book has no direct connection to flowers except in its title and in the design of the book cover which features a photograph of a painting called Blodyn.**

If you know that Blodyn is the Welsh word for flower, and you do now, you'll understand why the painting is called Blodyn.

But why is this book called Blodyn?

I think it's because Blodyn, the painting, is very special to me and the words in this book are special too. They say all there is to say about me and about the way I see the universe I am presented with.

Blodyn is neither plant nor animal, neither he nor she, yet she is both plant and animal. She is pure and raw and beautiful and animalistic and wild – she is part of who I am and I come here to honour her.

** Blodyn, by deRec: acrylic on board 520mm x 670mm, 2001

Stopping Stone

Here we have a stopping stone
a place to pause and be alone
Take it in your hand and stare
at nothing in particular
Rub it clean and roll it round
make it tumble on the ground
Chuck it, kick it, lob it high
watch it dropping from the sky
Let it rest, be on your way
thank it humbly for today
Tomorrow someone else will pause
have their day, and think of yours.

Even in Winter

Even in winter there are pools of light.
What is this doing to our collective psyche?
Changing the universal direction,
Scrambling the structure
of life.

How will the human organism survive?
In what form will we evolve?
To reach the stars outside,
We abandon the essence
of life.

In the future, if there is one,
We will be points of light,
Free-moving consciousness,
Pushing to the limits
of life.

After a While

Blackbirds, turning over frozen leaves
Mud frozen and crunching
Underfoot the feel of ice-cold winter
leaving its clean air in my chest
People around the bend in the path
Fenced out by green mesh
around the ministry's land
where my fathers added their hands
to mould and chisel on demand
How much longer? The question comes
For how many more days can we strip
this earth and burn and tear
down the trees, the lungs that care?
Then people, dogs and contact's made
a nervous moment, other eyes in the world
Eyes that seek recognition
Eyes that speak of disassociation
and always legs that carry
on, revolving, spinning
like a kicked ball
After a while the stubs and cans
of used up pleasures, so banal
that poor minds need to feel okay
for one more grey cold wasted day
The path peters out and ends
in road, where vehicles convey their load
Then from the path behind we hear
the adieu of some black bird.

February Again

The debris of last summer's sunflowers
Still alive onions
Hose still connected to the outside tap
and the fork still upright
where I plunged it last August

     – it's February again

Surprisingly
The wheel on the barrow still turns.

Hello Spring

It's no good pretending, lurking,
I can see you coming.
You can't help it, can you?
It's something you have to do,
whether you like it or not.
So stop hiding,
come out from under your shield of last year's leaves,
reveal yourself,
you are wanted,
needed.
Hah! With your cheeky yellow wink,
of course you know,
you were just teasing.
Well, you are –
here again.
Hello Spring.

Just a game

I won a fiver on the lottery last night
then I went to Swansea

The other day I spent a tenner on scratchcards
and won
nothing

Still Never Mind
It doesn't Matter
It's just a game

It's all a game.

Swans Sea Marina

Swans, fat on clumps of white bread.
Sea, beyond a grey wall.
Waves, pushing and dropping and rushing
on the early sand.

Red brick cliffs, hollow with people,
growing like slow teeth stained with oily water.
Artefacts, constructed by pygmy-slaves
for mental incompetents.

Glass, bubbled and trapped in a plastic tube.
Gulls, of course, in closed courtyards,
forbidden to peck, but still singing.
Seeing beyond the experience

A long rag shed, housing past pain.
Outside, the remembered seats.
No place to piss only complain
of swans and plump white clumps
on oily water.

National Poetry Day

Write a poem in 45 minutes he said
Who said?
Before midnight, he said
A poem before midnight?
Yes in 45 minutes he said
Easy
44 minutes he said
One is enough
Just one he said
Yes I said
It's done
That'll do, he said

Mumbling

I pause on a bridge
and watch the river,
with its load,
as it tumbles past my window,
and I often sigh.

I see the fields where I played,
and the people of that dream,
and I remember.
Sometimes I cry.

I stop on the corner;
watch the traffic,
as it trundles,
and I wonder,
where does it fly?

I cross the road and look over
at the river,
at its hurry,
at the way it keeps renewing,
at its lie.

There's no ending to this story,
just beginning,
as it falls
along its passage,
mumbling by.

A Glove Poem

Snug in the blanket you weaved yourself,
with a shedful of wood for the winter.
It's time at last to peek out;
to taste the colding air,
and to plan
for your future.

You will soar to the tops of the hill tonight,
held by a strong steel rope,
with a net of prudence,
and a cup of gold,
collected,
by stealth.

When your mother told you to get it made,
you had it made in the cradle.
You folded your blanket and tucked it away,
in a silverthread box;
kept it warm,
protected.

Somewhere you tripped on a worn-out skin,
in a place where you should not have been.
But all it did was remind you
to keep to the path;
to protect,
to survive.

It's not your fault that you want to be free.
It's always been part of your nature.
For you are a human like me,
and need to taste the moon
even though,
it's not cheese.

For all that, it's not the case that I hate.
I don't dislike your fluffy-coat any more
than the rain must fall.
Sparkling under the gloom,
I see
your humanity.

Spare me a moment to let me explain
why I think your success will be empty.
It's just a foray in the woods
with a piece of cotton
tied to your leg
for safety.

When the Hour Goes Back

When the hour goes back
it reminds me of another life
other lives
And there, when I looked out from different eyes
I saw the same things
but in a different hue
A colouring added by a careful hand
to create the right effect
Then it was warm and light
but it's easier now
to write in this cryptic way
Trying to paint the white bits
in a particular way.

At first, there seems to be
only dark purples
if you're lucky
otherwise
it's just black
and rather damp.

Then you remember the too-easy evenings
the too endless
days
And it takes a while
to adjust
to the new light
And then you settle for partial darkness
trying to believe
what they told you,
so long ago.

But you droop – like a dying sunflower
and can't even feel the light finger-touch
which is all you can get
at this time of year.

Then the hour's gone back
and it takes a few dark weeks
before you notice
a light of red
and a light of green
and a light of blue
and a light of white
placed in the middle
And you know
You Know.

On Walls

On walls
low brick walls
boys sit
and think
boys spit
and cover the tarmac
with white globules

In their rooms
they keep grime
proddable stuff
dark places
to hide futures

Go on – Try it.

A dog
a large brown dog
a large brown dog on a lead
going nowhere
but it doesn't care
try putting a wolf on a lead
and taking it nowhere
go on
try it.

A cow
a fat red cow
a fat red cow in a field
doing nothing
but it doesn't care
try putting a unicorn in a field
and giving it nothing
go on
try it.

A man
a tall white man
a tall white man in a suit
being no-one
but he doesn't care
try putting a gorilla in a suit
and making it no-one
go on
try it.

I am a Black Bird

I am a black bird,
shuffling, in the sun;
turning over old leaves
with my yellow beak.

I need to look you in your eyes;
need to find
where you hid the worms.
And don't give me any more
of those empty, brittle shells
of snails
long gone.

I know you know the lairs
of the slime-makers,
but your face is a bland blank mess
of colour and noise
that hides two pink worms,
and a pair of juicy white
maggots –
curled
into balls.

Before you came and dug
and dribbled
your bitter water,
I flew free.
recalled it all,
blinked, taking shots –
a frozen leaf,
a luscious grub,
pure rainwater in the shape
of your early foot.

Yes, I am a black bird
a silhouette
against the sun,
an almost
imperceptible
note
of what you've done.

Drowned in Light
(4 old men discussing paintings in an exhibition)

They are like flowers at the end of summer
They take their turn to disappear
Colours fade
Petals droop
Drop

They have shared their light with our world
A light that leaves a picture
On the silver of our memories
A light that cannot fade
It is caught
It still shines

There is so much of this light
so much, it is filling up the universe

Soon

We will all drown in light
and live forever.

A Morning Walk

Let's get it over with:
this bladder-emptying,
skin-scraping,
tooth-cleaning,
toilet-time.

Move on, get out –
walk.
The world wakes and
the accumulated, sense-gathered paradigm
descends,
and gives meaning to our memories.

We are balls of rubber,
wound tight,
in our special way,
containing the energy
that makes our unique life
lived.

See the girl in her shop
of hope;
she's hanging up her heart,
inviting the time-stealer –
not knowing
yet, the death of her dreams.

At the back of the pub,
overflowing with last night's yack,
the man with the yawn's,
emptying ashtrays.

He doubts his choices,
checks the curl of his eyebrow
in the mirror,
as he comes to full-consciousness
and becomes what he thinks he is.

An old man, selling without shame,
waiting for his dotage,
already dead with complaining.
Formed in a different reality,
when black was not white.
His acceptance of all things,
leads him to present
whatever is deemed truth
by a diseased society,
in his shop of conformity.
While he taps his irritation,
waiting for his liberation.

A peddler of incoherent techno-trash,
his salvation's chamber,
clanging with clutter.
His best hope,
the giving-up,
the inevitable failure,
inviting re-birth.

Faceless in the false-bright alleyway,
absorbing the sweat
of a thousand blotted lives –
the irreverent master

promises the neat-wrapped
quality-controlled existence.
Its obliteration,
the only condition,
that will satisfy.

And in the tidy china shop,
a crock of unasked for mediocrity –
putrefying.

You, submerged in slime,
sanitised, rinsed-out slobber,
hacking your way to the cemetery,
deaf to the whisper of death,
seek meaning in my eyes.
I, knowing only this life's
full reality,
confound your glance,
and we,
exchange
our memories.

Now you
continue
and I
return
to my taking-stock.

Dead Moths

dead moths under flowerpots
slug bitten beans
bluebottles in a shed
long boats with wheels removed
broken trailers, concrete debris
a house without a phone
five children in the window
the captain's all at sea
glossy covers laminated
bond paper
black text
bringing in the dosh
telephone calls enthusiastically received
messages received
by the score
organic bananas speckling
in the wooden bowl
forms everywhere – all around
books and wooden tables
plastic buttons
L.E.D.s
camera films
digital photos
spectacles
how full can a day be?

Game Over You Win

So you cracked it then
You won the game
You overcame the difficulties
and the random events
You made the most of your luck
and you played your hand well

And now its time to smile
and enjoy the prize of satisfaction
smile, damn you
you won didn't you?
didn't you?

Perhaps you realised
that there's more than one game
that this was a game in a series
and now it's best out of five
or something like that

Or maybe there are other games
or other levels
that you didn't see
other players in different divisions or leagues

Or maybe you finally realised
that it doesn't matter
whether you won
or you lost
it's only a game
after all

Game over
You win?

Ninetyfivefive

you know the score
in a movie
or a tv show
the flaws
small flaws
idiosyncratic flaws
twelve flaws
or just one
we're allowed to be flawed
it's ok as long as in the end
we're fucking good at our job
in my real life i'm an artex ceiling of cracks and
fissures
with some small redemption

it's kind of arse-backwards ain't it?

You're Fab

There are those that wake with still closed eyes
And grunt and hide and live in lies
They swallow anything that comes
And lay to rest with nothing done.

Then there are the ones that see
That live their own humanity
They show their beauty in the night
And when they leave they leave a light.

The Words in Me

i
On the cool May water
patient ducks do their duckly duty
and chilled out swans lurch
in almost imperceptible leaps.
One, a big one by the sound of its wings,
flies berserkly, its feet still in the water
behind the bushes,
where I lay with a girl in the long rushes.
A hard-nailed dog, paws stiff as death
chews a fluorescent tennis ball
and vaguely obeys the small man,
whose narrow dark eyes acknowledge,
but only out of duty.

The pond is not warm now.
Was it ever?
Even when the old works of
undulating metal disgorged its useless vigour.

This place is a place where times collide
and all roads cross.
My fathers, survivors though they were,
naturally,
thought they were here to stay,
thought they could walk on the water.

That pond, that cool May pond,
that clean green pond,
that home to dutiful ducks
and chilled out swans,
started with their sweat
and with their water.

The cross-ponds bridge, the tidy tarmac,
the grass, the dog shit, the drunken piss.
See – even now the waters come – even now
but with less pain.

An angry crow, helpless,
or it could be a rook,
anyway, it has a big yellow beak
and it craws loud and angry
at the new road and the thick-wheeled cycles
and the motorised wheelchair, and most of all
most of all, it shouts at the patient ducks.

ii
A dying pylon collapses, its corpse disintegrates.
The three parts of its giant insect body,
decomposing prey to the acetylene burners
and the maggot men with their big yellow jaws.

iii
A slow pad over the arc of the Pont d'Agen
to the tarmacked path, where the long rushes were
and a nervous coot, scoots, home to its dying mother.

iv
Like a lost turtle, out of place,
the ghost of my future is barely seen
by the thick meat frame and quick cold eyes
of men, protecting their brood,
with their stares.

I am alone, more akin to my dead father,
less at home than I was as a child,
even though then, I stole and lied
and cheated at cards,
when I could get away with it.

Without a dog, or a bike, or a young child,
or even a girlfriend,
I walk on purpose
even though I'm not going anywhere,
just crossing and looping
and thinking of then
and thinking of now
and thinking of then again,
as I avoid the cold sharp stares.

v
Polly the dog makes a nuisance of itself.
The little girl craws its name
like an angry black crow.
Her mother tugs, it's time,
time, it's always time to go.

vi
This is a moderate place
it hovers between then and now
between here and there
existing only because
of a random coming together
of the right sort of stuff
but it still hurts.

vii
Under the arc of the Pont d'Agen
cars flow; the scintillating heat
of their breath
settles on the new-made road,
and she sighs,
and she hides
her secret methods.
But she knows,
and she will
recover.

viii
It's time, and time again,
time to let the dreams
vaporise
and settle
and hide
in the black tarmac,
and wait
for a new reality.

I Saw Two Buzzards

I saw two buzzards soaring
nonchalantly
They swooped in a slow loop
lazily looking
Eyeing a small creature
A time of plenty
time to get fat
to flop lazily
on the warm draughts
Until the slow night.

Coruscation

Wooden seed contains the tree of life's
Essential fruit ensuring certain death.
The bite that unsheathed time's sharp-bladed knife,
Cut off humanity, left us bereft.
To Cox's, Braeburns, Bramley apple pies,
Genuflecting to scientists' whims
Alar, phosphates and insect-killing sighs,
Genetic changes, false gods, crazy things.
The end of all we know's in sight again,
Where, when and then and now and all is past,
When love and death and life come to an end.
There you and I will be as one at last.
    But while we strive to bear the stench of bliss,
    My breath is coruscated by your kiss.

We Live in Such Erudite Times

Men in Afghanistan burst
buddhas with a yell.
Politicians, even decent ones
play with penthouses
overlooking Hyde Park.
Farmers cry
over dead sheep,
and McDonald's sponsor cancer research.

Autumn's Breath

Hello autumn.
It's good to see you again.
We missed your damp blowing.
We need: your field-wide energy;
to breathe your lullaby,
before winter drops
its dark drape
and wraps us safe,
asleep,
until
it's spring.

Tossers
(derived from the play Tossers)

(i)
The cheap virginal plates are stained with spuds,
Scrubbed and boiled to soft green bloody pulp;
A fiction, fantasy, implicit trust;
Nothing to see, to feel, beyond the clumps,
Of cloud that is impossible to touch.
Then lumpy, soggy, milky hidden mud,
Or maybe salad tainted by the slug,
Whose silver slime betrays the adult blush.
After, a bowl of floury lardy mulch,
Drowned in sweet and sickly yellow stuff,
That fakes the taste of real wooden struts,
And gives a nourishment that's not enough.
Under the blanket breaks a little beam,
Uncut connection to the golden stream.

(ii)
It could have been true, we could have won,
had that tuft of grass kicked the other way,
had that foul disease not spread,
had that child been born another day,
were it not that Gandhi was then dead.

It should have been us, we should have won,
had that referee looked the other way,
had that thunderstorm not spread,
had that summer stayed another day,
were it not the seed we sought was dead.

It would have been right, we would have won,
had that gust of wind blown the other way,
had that dull flat note not spread,
had that chaos stayed another day,
were it not the child in us was dead.

(iii)
In the end, the child in us kills its creation.
With its brooding resentment
It has lain there, knowing, waiting
For the moment when it can strike.
For the child hates the blobby body,
And the wrinkled face,
And the twisted stomach.
The child is king,
The creator and the destroyer.
The child is dying
To end the folly
Of our old age.
A clean cull,
A neat chop,
And freedom
To be born again.

REFRESHMENTS AFTER THE MEETING IN A TIDY ROOM IN A VILLAGE IN WALES – A SMALL COUNTRY IN EUROPE

A rectangle of round men
represent, aspire
to impress
to allow or distort
the wishes
that bubble
through the decomposing hay.
They nod and falter
mumbling
the song
they have learnt
from their fathers.
Somewhere else
slight children
leave small convex scars
the length of a breath,
– for coffee
– for dainty biscuits
and a good night's rest.
Ah – it has been a dutiful day.

The Back Door

The back door rots as I sit in the sun, and
it will rot when I close it tight against
the dark and the cold wet winter.

I see the woodlice, buttons with legs, harmless
things they said. They carry it away -
the rotting wood.

Organic carrots made with blood, washed
clean by the cold water drawn from the river,
and steamed with beans

A short-lived shrew, its head crushed, lies,
along with its family, in a circle on
the lawn

The old man is waiting, not long now, and
he can take his place near the fire and
fall asleep without fuss.

A lazy swallow dies as the day
yawns and caresses the fading flower bed
with its farewell.

And in the end it is only now and
there is a desperate need for sleep.

Waiting Haikus

haikus, things to do
when you're bored outside a pub
and friends don't turn up

autumn is delayed
by a burst of summer sun
birds take advantage

near summer's end
yellowing leaves start their trip
to the brown gutter

like a dance they swirl
on the pavements, in the road
then they separate

noisy crows in trees
saying goodbye to the sun
when it's gone, they stop

on the bark of trees
forests of green moss congeal
it's complicated

Would They?

If fish had evolved as much as human beings
would they feel the same sadness?

If donkeys could talk would they complain
about the pain in their kidneys?

Would man-eating tigers hang dead
humans upside down in cold warehouses?

How many ring-tailed lemurs would it
take to replace a light bulb?

Would monkeys have mosques
and chinchillas churches?

Would elephants cremate their dead?

And sing songs at weddings?

Would they?

Would they?

Distances Disappear in the Dark

Distances disappear in the dark
somewhere a train melts the night
and I sit in my secret place

On the streets
you can see the lights
and a car screeches its loneliness

I like to sit and speak to you
when no one else is listening,
hoping you'll stay awake too

There is though a wind blowing
and in another country
my friend is asleep

It makes me feel good to taste your breath
and finish the day
in an appropriate way

Passing a Day

Dum-tee-dum-tee-dummm-tee
I'm a little monnn-key
sitting on a biig-tree
Dum-tee-dum-tee-dummm-tee

This is what I see
This is what I see

I see a cloud
I see a sky
I see a parrot
flying by
It winks at me

This is what I see

I see a branch
another tree
Another monkey
looks at me
It winks at me

This is what I see

I see a stone
a river-bed
a long-legged bird
nods its head
It winks at me

This is what I see

I see the dark
below my bed
I see its dankness
see its dead
It winks at me

This is what I see

I see the sun
It shares its light
It leaves its shadow
in the night
It winks at me

This is what I see

Dum-tee-dum-tee-dummm-tee
I'm a little monnn-key
sitting on a biig-tree
Dum-tee-dum-tee-dummm-tee

This is what I see
This is what I see

About the Journey

It's not finished yet, this journey
that began when the first eyes
opened, to a universe unknown.
When the composition
was a mystery.
When colours melded
into one space-less blur.
Before the images resolved,
and a birth shook the world.

Then, its end assured,
it began.
First, the breathed air,
creating oneness,
within and without.
The stream flowed and joined
'til all subsumed
into the universal consciousness.
The spectrum is endless,
turning the continuum,
everywhere at once,
every-when here.
The probes extended and tasted;
its paradigm revealed
in sense-full tasteful wholeness.
Mobility unstuck itself,
and flickered as it shifted,
catching here, the deep
black depth, here the bright
blinding blandness,
and in between –
The lie bought and lived.

Death sought and given.
And always that awareness,
the pain, the bliss, of breathing.
That always uncertain sureness,
on the surface only crawling,
blind concentrated sprawling.
Caught in that ripple
of here-ness, of now-ness,
of whatever-there-will-be-ness.
The structure of the story,
revealed, flamed breath.
Eyeballing creatures with
hollow hopelessness unneeded.
No desire for enlightenment,
no wish for comprehension.
Just eat and live and sleep it,
the others they can keep it,
but no,
on a need to know basis.
Unacceptable stasis.
It doesn't end, because,
there's no beginning either.
A fusion of confusion,
a chaotic sensibility.
As if it emptied of itself.
It only needs a slender thread,
unbroken and unbreakable,
else nothing, void-ness.
Beckoning the flames,
womb warmth, comfort.
Home, there is no succour
for the essential consciousness.

The pleasing reflection,
dull though it is,
hints at perfection,
allows a sneak glimpse,
of the structure that's not.
So brilliant, so blank,
it'll never be found,
'cos it never existed.
There's nowhere to go and there's nothing to see.
There's no time to show and there's no place to be.
So, having struggled to kick,
to breathe, and to spit.
Now, meek acceptance,
overcomes reluctance,
and begins in truth,
to explore, to carry,
the burden of humanness
across the bleak surface of a world,
that gives a little,
less, the more hope
the more pain.
And out of this splattered pattern,
comes a kind of knowing,
a period to grow.
To continue and resolve.
To solve and understand.
The hopeless, lifeless mess.
We make our own redemption
by flailing against conformity,
until tired, until rest,
until time sleeps and
until the endless void stops.

Then a flash of clarity.
Then a brief welcome,
to what it is we live,
what it is we give.
Of fading faculties.
Of re-submerging.
Of re-emerging.
And always the thin,
the tenuous, the fragile
humble beam unbroken.
The truth never spoken.
Do not expect an ending.

Scum

The Evening Post today reported
That itinerants and vagrants
Had set up camp behind Oxfam
"It was a rubber glove and peg job"
On another page
a homelessness book was launched
in Swansea
While the dirty scum
made tents on the barbed wire.

Dreamers

Only the hawk knows the secrets
its eyes devour the comings and goings
the togetherness
The landscape is a pin-sharp blade of grass
or is it a blur of green
a rush of barely-disturbed air
and the blood
the life blood

But people are not hawks
and they can't see the same things
they can't glide like a dandelion head
they can't plummet like an anchor
they can only dream
and dream they do
they dream.

Poems for competitions

Impact
Delivery
Reception
That's how it comes
That's how it goes
As if from a parallel world where:
You are a Goddess
And I am not your lover
But I am
I am!

###

It is a temporal illusion
This life
It is a smudge on a lens
This time
we spend together is already a smile
at a memory

###

An expedition is needed
A visit to another place
Where there is other fruit
Hanging – waiting
It is needed
Wanted even
But it's not ripe
Yet

###

Time is one thing
Place is another –
thing
They come together
in unique spits of meaning
endless variegations
to make a life
a generation
a culture
an age
a star-cycle
a galaxy-wide pulse
of meaning
in an infinity
of universes
and inside
inside
there is Love

###

Midwinter Solstice

The last wisp of hope
and then
the turn
undercurrents
dragging me home
tossing – not drowning
the pull of the sea
with its warmth
its cold depth
of meaning to me

Sunday Night

Sunday night, alone
A place to empty pockets
A place to dream
Before the beginning again.

Sunday night – boring – dread of tomorrow
Guilt of not doing
Lonely tiredness – hunger on a full stomach
Quiet anticipation
The rumble of the motorway
still, in the distance.

The click clock tick of the click clock clock
The shuffle on the kitchen floor
The dampened murmur of the Sunday night arts
programme
The car getting colder waiting
for the simple turn of a key

Last chance to dream
The full silence
Full of hisses, rumbles
yet to come
and those already gone
The weak end of the week end
and the start of tomorrow always.

War Planes Over Wales

In peaceful times
they are nuisances
microscopic post-it notes
speckling in the sky.

Now, they fly low
and are angrier
hand size, land size shadows
drawing in the eye.

In the dark

In the late dark, a visitor
From a summer, long departed
Teased from winter's slumber
Deceived by central heat
And a wall to wall mat
A microdot of consciousness
For a moment sharing awareness
As it slips across my clutter

Care in the Community

I saw an old man sitting on a bench
breathing the traffic-polluted air in huge gulps
snatching puffs of cigarettes in between
His feet dancing on the ground beneath the seat
Hours, he was there
Hours, he is there
every day
Cared for in the community.

Moth

Until it falls, burnt out and dead,
it must persist to weave its thread
It's flimsy body seeks the light,
that's always somewhere in the night.

Black Cat

I saw him chew a frog with glee
his yellow eyes assessing me
I saw him die, his kidneys gone
An obligate carnivore done.

Little Dog

Behind those eyes a simple soul
Obliged to eat and piss and growl
It needed recognition too
To leave its mark on every shoe.

Things you forget about Summer
(When it's Winter)

Low-flying aeroplanes.
Flies.
Buzzing strimmers.
Bees.
Buzzers.

Nothing New

There's nothing new under the sun
and there never was
Like the old woman with her hair
in a bun
She's not new because
she's old

A friend once told me that she'd found
an undiscovered treasure
A hard-shelled beetle, small and round
and it give her pleasure
so I lied

I said that's good, I like your style
I like the way you look
I like your singing and your smile
the way you hold your book
and she cried

Another time I met a man
with a face as round as peach
He kept his eyeball in a can
He said he'd found it on a beach
in Ireland

I asked him when his parents died
Where were they buried now
He told me they were still alive
his mother was a dairy cow
that laughed.

Reporters in Time

It's the beginning of the universe
and I'm here – live
It's difficult to see
through the cosmic smog
I haven't yet caught
a glimpse of God

What I can tell you, is
it's not what you think
un-describable emptiness
dumb-blind nothingness
not very interesting really
back to the studio

Well, we'll return there
to the beginning of time
where space emerges
after we visit
our man at the end
where even light bends

Well, hello, I think I can see
the start of the end
The Almighty's big joke
I can almost hear
him laughing
But it's quiet and bleak
now

We'll rejoin the start
when we've sorted the glitches
For now our correspondent reports
on the bit in-between
where there have been developments
over to you

Hello – here's a montage
of sub-atomic particles
and everlasting energy
where planets and suns
spin in the firmament
and creatures ingest
the material

I witnessed it all
from the first ball
from the first run
of the sperm
to the egg

I heard of a place
where, despite incontrovertible evidence
a consciousness formed
a reality

Until we realised and came to accept
inconsistency
unbelievability
randomness wins
every time

Now of course with our knowledge
with our celluloid snare
with our sealed-up existence
we make sense of the fog
There must be a God
We'll soon know

Thank you for watching
for hearing for feeling
Thank you for tuning
your mind to our meaning

Let us feed off your blood
and infest your being
give us your energy
for a while

How is it looking
over there in Creation?
How are things shaping
in the time of Destruction?
What can you tell us?
What can you see?
Over to you
let's begin

Well thank you studio
but there's nothing to say
nothing to dwell on
apart from the grey

I'd love to say fireworks
and mind-numbing sound
the biggest of bangs
Divine Light all around
But in the beginning
it all seems to me
like a day-trip to empty
eternity

And here at the end
there's nothing as well
there's little to see
less even to tell

As soon as we get something
we'll return to the scene
for now relax and enjoy
the music we made
earlier

Observe the patterns
in the grains of the sand
feel the breath of fire
on your hand
Hang on!
Something's happening
at both ends
at once

Yes I'm happy to tell you
the beginning's begun
The greyness unfolds
there's something, someone

Wait just a moment
the view's getting good
there's something beyond me
not yet understood

And me, all the waiting's
paid off as it goes
the end is upon me
it's all making sense
the black hole is calling

I'll have to go in
Bear with me a moment

It's getting exciting
it's finally here
the camera's ready
the instruments tuned
the sensors are waiting
it's gonna be soon

Ah! The speakers are crackling
The pictures are dim
There's a technical problem
Cut back to singing

While we're all waiting
for the techies to work
let's check the developments
back here on Earth

We started with nothing
began to explode
absorbing the energy
our purpose exposed

And now we've reviewed
and picked apart all
There's no more to say
there's no one to call

We'll wait for reports
. . . .

Ah!
Now there's life in the links
the picture is clear
The message is simple
there was nothing to fear

Our man at the end
meets his very best friend

Who am I

Who am I?

Where do I put my coat before dinner?

Under the stairs?
Maybe,
but it's already full of crap
and other people's coats,
and mine won't fit there,
and even if it did,
it wouldn't look right.

How about in a box in the boot of my car?
But what's the point of that?
No one will see it.

Perhaps I should just throw it on the settee?
What d'ya think?
Nah, the trouble with that
is that there are already
people sitting there,
and they'd probably get annoyed
and wouldn't understand anyway.

And it's no good telling me to hang it up,
'cos all the pegs are full
and anyway, my coat smells
and occasionally
offends.

So, the way I see it
I've got two choices:
1 – Don't bring a coat
2 – Don't go to dinner

Number 1 is not an option
because my coat is all I have
and I have to carry it everywhere
except perhaps in bed.

And no 2?
Maybe?
Yes – that's what I'll do,
I won't go to dinner
I'll just pop into the Chinese takeaway
on the way home
and grab a bag of starch and goo.
That'll keep me going until tomorrow.

Weird – Me?

If I was to sit down
in the aisle
in the supermarket,
adopt the Lotus
and meditate,
people would think
I was weird.
Yet if I was a
Buddhist monk
in a monastery
people would think
I was weird
if I didn't.

Power Cut

Quiet – the clock actually ticks
I can hear it now in the dark
I haven't noticed that
before
Not that I can remember
even in the sometimes
small times I keep
alone
to the buzzing of the
fridge and the awful
fluorescent long light
and the rage of
the bundling unfinished
letters to my lover
She comes sometimes too
in that full dark
Showing off her unthinking
pleasures
And when the full bowl
breaks and falls to bits
I cannot still hear
the added energy draining
soft regular beat of
her heart.

Robin

Pecking up the scraps of summer
He comes hopping –
and perching –
in cute poses;
Makes you wish you had a camera, ready.
Pictures of Robins
do well at Christmas.

Jackdaw

Where I live
There are families
of Black Birds
They live on our roofs
and ramble on our lawns
They never stop nodding
and they make you feel
cynical.

Turkey

These are birds too,
even though
they're cajoled
and crammed
and clipped
and co-erced
until they bleed for us,
at Christmas.

Gull

A varied people
Albatross-sized
or sharp white darts
tipped with black.
They argue a lot,
eat anything you throw at them,
and try to tell us
about the weather.

Duck

They are mostly seen
on man-made ponds,
and amuse us,
occasionally,
with their courting.
You somehow
feel obliged to them
and wish you'd brought
some bread.

On the River

Swans duck on the river
and ducks swan on the river
on the river

Stella cans (empty ones)
and lesser beers
on the river

Wood, fashioned
people in shorts
on the river

Sun, light, sunlight
slick oil
on the river

On the river – early night.

How to See

Look, I can point at something
like a child points at cars
I can learn to draw
and use an arrow
a long arrow
with the appropriate sized head
in a powerpoint demonstration
I can learn to draw
Your Attention.

Look, I can show you things
describe the structure of the innerspiral
of the cochlea
and even have a go
at describing
its function.

Look, I can take your hand
and drag you to the window
I can pull aside the curtain
and I can keep your
eyes open
with matchsticks.

There are many things I can show you
too many things
Perhaps
Instead
Perhaps
I can teach you how to see.

I am the moon

I am the moon. I have always been the moon. I will always be the moon. My heart beats with cool light. I move my thoughts over the blue emptiness. I vibrate with blue emotion.

There is no thing except the cool blue. There is no place except the cool blue. There is only the cool blue.

I am the moon. I do not feel. I do not see. I do not hear. I am the moon.

There is no thing. Nothing. I am the moon.

I am the blue moon. I am alone.

"Did you say something?"
"Did you say something?"
"Who are you?"
"Who are you?"
"Who am I?"
"Who am I?"

"I am the moon."
"I am the moon."

I am the blue moon.
I am alone.

"The moon looks blue tonight."
"No it doesn't, it is white. The sky is blue"
"The sky has no colour. The moon has no colour"
"It's the light from the sun. It has no light itself."

"It's late. It's cold."
"The moon affects the sea."
"And me."
"Everyone."
"Always."

"Take my hand, it's dark."
"Your hand is cold."
"Warm enough. You are not alone."
"I love you."
"I love you."

"It's a beautiful night."
"A beautiful sight."
"A beautiful light."

"Let's go home."

"Goodnight moon."
"Goodnight moon."

"Take my hand."

"I love you."
"I love you."

"Let's go home."

"You are with me now."

I am the moon. I am the blue moon. I am alone.

Poem Police

These are my words and I'll do what the . . . . . .

The rest of this poem has been deleted . . .

C E N S O R E D

C E N S O R E D

C E N S O R E D

C E N S O R E D

C E N S O R E D

C E N S O R E D

C E N S O R E D

C E N S O R E D

C E N S O R E D

C E N S O R E D

Every moment

Every day
Every drop
Every minute
Every where
Every second
Every step
Every thing
Every time
Every way
Every one
Every breath
It all counts

Where Have You Been All Summer?

Ah.
Here you come, all bounding and smiling,
through the fading grasses of Autumn.
I'm back, you say.
I'm back to light up the coming darkness.
I'll see you through to Christmas at least,
and probably to the early days of Spring.

But why? I ask.
Why did you desert me when the wind got warmer?
We could have had such a breeze,
you and me and the sunshine.
There was such a lot of daylight.
We could have danced, we could have sung,
We could have had fun.

Ah.
You say. You didn't need me then,
you lived in the sunshine, with the birds.
You had time to live, time to love,
time to be yourself.
And now the daylight gets less,
and I will be your friend – again.

Autumn Leaves

How many trees are on the Earth
How many leaves
How many stars are in the sky
How many moons
How many days are in a life
How many breaths
Enough
Just enough!

Autumn Trees

The tree knows where to grow
The stream knows where to flow
The breeze knows when to sigh
The leaf knows when to die

Odds and Ends

1
Bites of philosophy
Flakes of meaning
Preserve them
For midwinter
Treats for the psyche
Bon-bons for the soul
4

2
Along the way
I sometimes stay
At your house
And I'm glad
Thanks

3
A wave, a smile,
a little twinkle in an eye,
remind me –
I'm alive.

4
the emperor's new poem
isn't it fab
isn't it bad
isn't it sad
isn't it mad
isn't it glad
no it isn't

5

Feardrops seep in
late at night
when the world is cold
and I am old
tumbling towards eternity.
Before it gets too dark
when the world is bleak
and I am weak.
But then, you smile,
and all is well,
for a while.

6

I can only tell you what I know
for certain, that's not much.
Just that awareness lingering there,
sensitive to your touch.

7

An age where you could be young or you could be old,
or you could be something in between.
A phase of light illuminates,
the bleak rich second of the scene.
Here's a man I used to know pushing a trolley
filled with grandchildren.
Over there's an older friend,
starting a new relationship.

8

a thought given freedom
for you to interpret as freely as you please
makes sense to the hundred million monkeys with
their olivettis

9

All the sadness in the world started there,
In my green heart.
When I looked on you
For the first time.
That's when I spoke your name
And shuddered with joy.
That's when it all began,
And when it ended.

10

Note to a trainee slaughterperson:

Before you kill a lamb:
You must perform this quick simple check.

1: Stick your fingers in its mouth.
2: Yank.
3: Examine the condition of its baby teeth.
4: Check its age against the diagram.
5: If in doubt, call your supervisor.

11
Early morning gaps
In the fabric of a life
Divine inconsistencies
Add meaning

12
I'm not a fucking farmer, right
I'm not a fucking choirboy either, obviously
I'm Welsh, but I'm not fucking stupid
I was brought up on a council estate but
I'm not a bastard or a fucking criminal

13
Too many poets
too many fucking poets
too many poets, fucking
with my mind

14
Sunlight
glinted on the water
and I drank it

15
The wind is nothing
a shift of air
and water is elemental
and filled with dolphins

16
Canna a man have too many boids?
Little boids canna sing
Little goils canna pee
Standing up.

17
Poetry in Pencil?
It'll last long enough
to prove its worth.
Fading or evolving
into something more permanent.

18
Too many summers have gone
Too many winters have come
Remember this when you dance in the rain

19
We are One

wool snags on a wire
shakes
in the wind

light glints on a raindrop
drips
to the stream

20
You are there
and I am here.
But it's different from your perspective.

21
They are one-offs
ad-hoc gifts
letters
l e t t e r s
unique collections
meant to fragment
leaving a sweet note

22
Last night's potatoes
boiled too quickly
went to mush
and spread
like a bloom of summer's shadow

23
Clever things
cry at night
remembering
a future
the only fruit
a deep orange candle
shaped like a ball

24

A vibrant orange
hazy with heat shadows
the green richer somehow
crystal water
clear drops
shaking with glee
it's a calendula

25

Stainless steel ashtray
Sun glinting bright through the ash
Cigarette burns out

26

Leaves falling quickly
Turning brown in the weak sun
Blown into fat piles

27

The real meaning of Christmas
In the night
when day is at its most distant
the lights of green and red and white

28

Before bird bites
Spider slows
Tasting air

29
in the nettles
fallen apples
slug-eaten

30
wind in trees
steps in gravel
path home

31
Leaf on mud
Sun on face
Absorbed

32
Small cars carry important people
Large cars are mostly empty
because people are all the same size
    -    approximately

33
I thought it was green
most biros are not – of course
but it was blue
It was only a
trick-of-the-light.

The News Today

Terrorists.
Cancer.
Scroungers.
Migrants.
Murder.
Rape.
Death.
Hate.
Killing.
Slavery.
Ooh look, a player is kicking.
Ooh look, a popstar is kissing.
Ooh look, a prince is kidding.

No one reads

No one reads poetry,
except poets,
English Literature undergraduates,
and some academics.
(though these are mostly the same people)
No one reads poetry,
unless they have to,
or think they should
for their career.
(usually academic – sometimes journalistic)
If you follow a few rules,
show you understand,
you're not a charlatan,
you know the form,
you can be a poet too.
You then acquire mystical powers,
and you are allowed to judge,
to evaluate and assess,
to stamp your approval,
and you realise
that's what you wanted all along.

On a Broken, Worn Out, Cheap, Plastic, Cigarette Lighter

(i)
Oil processed, metal mined,
Gas released, so refined;
Cog turning, flint burning;
Ergonomically designed.

(ii)
reflections on a cigarette lighter:
distorted – not much.

(iii)
Shall I compare it to a source of light?
Or shall I simply call it flaming junk?
When it was new it struck and lit all right.
But now it's just a useless, lifeless hunk.

Of plastic, metal and of gas composed,
A man made thing to do the job of fire.
It might be clever if I juxtaposed,
The foundry's rush and a heavenly choir.

Singing its song it lit up many nights,
But now it's gone and ever will reside,
On the council tip with the other shite.
Silting the globe, why did it have to die?

Do not believe its life has been in vain,
'Cos from the dump it will rise once again.

(iv)
The thing is like a stick of light.
It is a bite of frost.
Its lion's roar, its breath so bright,
A broken beam, it's lost.

(v)
Fruit of mans' hand,
We don't understand,
How much you demand.

(vi)
There was a young lighter from Spain,
Who sparked time and time again,
'Til one day it fucked up;
No more gas it chucked up.
And now it's a piece of useless non-degradable landfill.

(vii)
(The Sick Lighter)
O lighter you ail!
The invisible gas,
That seeps from the earth,
In barely a flash,

Has left for the good
Of emptiness;
And its secret power
Does no more caress.

(viii)
Translucent plastic
Without a spark,
You were fantastic,
We had a lark.

But now it's all over;
And not before time.
Served like a lover;
Like a friend of mine.

(ix)
Fire breathing monster gone.
Plastic body all alone.
Lying on the kitchen floor.
I should have chucked you long ago.

(x)
A lighter you are;
A delicious tool,
Filled with flaméd gas.
A finite amount
Of breath to give;
To burn like the sun,
'Til your job's done.
Then what?
Return to the Earth.
Settle to rest,
Your exoskeleton.
And quietly de-compose.

But you're not the body,
So empty, devoid;
You are the fuel,
Now re-deployed.

(xi)
Dearly beloved,
We are gathered here together,
To represent an artefact -
A useful tool,
Dug up from the earth,
Designed by the Maker.
Put together
The molecules,
Thank Newton,
Thank Bell,
Thank Socrates,
And you might as well
Thank God.
But now it's time,
To begin the process
Of disassociation,
Of flying away,
Of re-emerging,
Re-Use,
Re-organisation.
Rest-in-Peace.

Busy Birds

Birds busy being
Busy birds being
Being busy birds
Birds being busy
Birds Being Busy Being Busy Birds

Always Singing

As the light is increasingly hidden
by the low grey clouds and longer shadows
inside, it's time to rest, to raid the
pantry under the stairs
and discover the precious knick-knacks you
put away in the active summer.
The days, like the gathering get shorter
and sink like the hard shells of crabs
in the mud.
But they're still there, always singing,
reminding us that there's
another tide
to come.

The double-edged explosion of life

In September I spent a lot of money.
I don't know why but it still hurts in December.
Perhaps it's the way the blood
drains and drips down the drain
and drips until, until
the world, before you know it, has
cheated you again.
Life cheats and promises
everything but in the end
delivers the only gift in its power –
That's what happens when the curtains
let in too much light – like they did
the night of the crescent moon when
Venus shone in its cradle and
if I am inside a room
with curtains drawn
and Venus shines
beyond the clouds –
What do I do?
How do I know?
What method is there to
communicate with stars?
Perhaps I should send
a missive, in a plain
brown envelope with a
false address and second name.
I may deliver a reciprocal wink,
I'm sure they can see me.
But, I'm inside the darkened room
looking for Venus in the wrong place
and going to bed with a sigh
after midnight
every night.

If we were rich

If we were rich, would we still have a table like this?
A table covered in the most recently used bits of shit?
Like scissors and glasses and ashtrays and tips.
Like candles and radios and needles and sticks.

There's last Tuesday's mailshots and yesterday's news.
There's this week's TV guide and half a pair of shoes.
A table that's creaking and sagging with clues.
Yes, we'd still have a table like this – it's the truth.

A Visit to Margam Steelworks

FIRST IMPRESSIONS

Roads meandering
Imposing structures
Imposing structure
Meandering roads

Giant Nostrils
Disgorging Clouds
Winds disturbing
Black noxious dust

Railway tracks
Slow-down bumps
Black puddles
Yellow jacks

Distance
Two miles
Maybe three
Lives Lived

Bad
Smell
Taste
Sound

Sight.

#

FAT FLIES

Fat flies in the portacabin office
Cheeky flies
Flies with confident looks
Licking their feet on
The mayonnaise roll

Un-noticing she eats
and she talks
about her chalet
in the South of France
and about how
these days they fly
instead of drive
It's not because
they're getting older
it's because
they get more time
in the sun
because
they get there quicker

Later –
there is a smell of silicon
and a metal can
spits its guts
into the atmosphere

The flies go away
for another day
but it would have been better
if she'd done it before lunch
long before

The humans cough for a bit.
Then go home.

#

PAVAROTTI'S PIPES

Pipes as wide as Pavarotti
and as long as –
The Royal Variety Performance
carrying
"Toxic Gas"
in their twists and turns

They arch the road
and arrogant sea birds
tip toe on top of them,
it could be a sign of rain
but then this place
is very close to
the sea anyway,
so you'd expect gulls

In some factory somewhere
there is a man
hacking and scraping
creating a pipe
big enough for Pavarotti
and no doubt
dreaming
about his coming holiday
in the sun
on the beach
by the sea
Side.

#

BLEATING

Seagulls bleating
in their particular way
On the roof
Inside a crazy man
but a controlled craziness
and only during
work hours
or sometimes down the pub.
Bleating – like a sheep
Bleating – and his companion laughing
and saying
"You DO have to be mad to work here".

But he's not listening –
this bleating man.
He's too busy talking –
about agricultural shows
and how he's booked a holiday
to attend one
in Pembrokeshire

And he takes the piss
out of his colleagues
on the phone
accusing them
of
bringing
the Hot Mill to a stop
because they made cups of tea
for all and sundry
Because taking the piss is part of the process

He's got to go
he sighs
to the agricultural show
because
he says: "I need to buy."

and who can blame him
because
after forty-odd years
of
wasting his humanity
on this shit
he needs to put in
a holiday request form
and either die
or go to shows and buy.

#

PHONES ARE FOR PLEASURE TOO

The temp with the smooth skin
glides into the office
she is young
with clean hair
and her voice is soft –
soft but tainted already
with this toxic life
and I'm sitting
at the keyboard
pretending
to work
while the virus
checker's checking
their computer
on my behalf

And a fat man of thirty-odd
comes into the office
with that
red-faced energy
you see sometimes
in fat men of thirty-odd

He's come to pick up a mobile phone
so the company
can keep in touch
and he turns it in his hand
like a nest-fallen chick
and he shrugs –
he doesn't like it
it feels too rubbery
and it looks too modern

But the girl with the smooth pink cheeks
takes a fancy
to its newness
and particularly likes
its polyphonic ringtones
that match
the lightness
of her skin

And she remarks that:
half of the company's mobile phones
are being used for pleasure

And the fat man laughs
as he imagines
but still refuses
to take the phone.

\#

THE AIR IS STALE BUT
WE'RE STILL BREATHING

The air on the landscape seems stale
but it's just the smell of the coal dust
and the remnants of toxic gas
disturbed by the wind from the sea
something they cannot control
despite the man-high fans
and the mile-long ducting
So they have to live with it

Because the rulers of the world
can continue with their
papers and reports
and keep pretending
that the peace
can be shattered
by a tiny terrorist
when they know that
it would take a nuke
the size of Swansea
to make a dent.

And in their hands
they hold the power
with a pen
a piece of paper
This place could die
Today
at the behest
of the global controllers.

Outside in October

The stems of the bamboos
in my neighbour's garden
are tall and waxy cream.
Their leaves like the bad hair
of an animated villain.
They sway like an armoury
of thin spears;
rattle, sometimes, in the wind.
It's a small innocent valley,
where the crabplant
and the blonde-haired pampas
jostle with potatoes;
buried like eggs of ants
in well-tilled mounds,
dissipating,
like mist, evaporating,
under the sun.
Betrayed, their fragility stalls,
and I expect to see
a black-and-white giant
panda
on the lawn.

And the Light

In the slimy stem bases
of wet bamboo
a vibrancy of greys
and greens
and blacks

Where lights spark
bringing to mind
the colour of a dark pond

A compost
an organic compost
made of dissolving
matter

and the light
and the light
the lightness of
a young
tom
cat
purring.

You know

I can sit on a riverbank
in the rain
and see the wetness
feel slime
hear water
taste dampness
slithering
alive with dust creatures
smelling like old black olives
I can do that
I can sit on a chair
in a room
an orange room
an orange room
where there were
rivers
and raindrops
and slimy grey creatures
and glow
in the warm
in the dry
feeling
touching
seeing
hearing
sensing
nothing
but
life.

New Friends

It was worth the wait
He caught a juicy slowworm
Though its skin looked
a bit hard to me

It was during the first cut
of the year of the lawn
and 4 jackdaws
were stalking me

I'd left it late
Mid-May
Far too late for some –
those pedantic gardeners
who spray – roses

It took him a few seconds
to clamp the wriggler
in his beak
I wonder if he's still
digesting it?
Like a python with a goat.

The grass is still growing
- anyway.

The Stream Outside

The stream outside flows unsteadily
it leaves smooth stones
and damp earth.
Just the right environment
for smidgeons of consciousness
that enjoy
smooth stones
and damp earth.

But it doesn't really go anywhere
drying up – as it does
before it reaches the
mud banks
of the estuary
another environment
where mud-loving bugs
and crabs
that will eat anything
meet surreptitiously
after dark
or in the shadows
of the day.

After the storm

There is a puddle in my garden.
In the puddle
There is next door's trousers
They are dark and grey
and meant for chapel
or officiating
at funerals
The legs
they normally contain
are old now
but still roadworthy
just about
After the storm
he is smiling
even though
he has to re-wash
his trousers
There's at least
half a dozen
ceremonies
left
in them
And maybe
more in him
but he's not so sure
so he won't buy
a new pair
just
yet

He doesn't want to rob his grandchild.

Now and Then

You have to let
them run
sometimes
Even if they fall

Look – it's like this -
even everyone
Clever bastards even
the cleverest ones
can only guess
anyway
so they – (the runners)
are as well-equipped
as anyone
to do anything
because nobody
knows
least of all
you.
So – let them run
sometimes
even if they fall.

What Do People Want

What do people want?

Things and things
like bread
like peanut butter
like green beans from Africa
and coffee
like cars
computers
shoes (theses are v. popular)

Sleep is important
Food of all kinds
(except GM)
Rest (Sleep especially)

Company they want
They want to share and care
(or be cared for (or both))

What do people want?

Shelter
Freedom
(From too much heat or too much cold)
Freedom
To come and go
To choose
or to just be/do

People want other people

Rose Petal

I have a rose petal in my hand
it is pink and feels kind of waxy
The colour fades towards the base
where there is yellow
it has a central spine
and there are lines scored in a fan
it's underside is pinker but less perfect
with grey blemishes in groups
it smells of scented soap
and tastes like sweet lettuce
The reason I have this petal
is because I tore it from the plant
recklessly disregarding
its primary purpose
and now to assuage the guilt
I have to make use of it
So I'll rub it in my hand
let its molecules of perfume and colour
rest on my skin
I'll squeeze it until it bleeds
then share its remains with the world

Under the Stone

it's damp under the stone
and life can live there
it's dark under the stone
and light can shine there
it's cold under the stone
and love can grow there
it's a habitat

An environment is where you live
and love and grow
it's where you glow
it's here
it's where you belong

mish-mash

a mish mash of cultures like boils on a bum erupting
into a wasteland of wasted lives where the dogs shit on
the pavements and the gravel as the lonely or mad
owners sigh in the dark of a december night passing
scurrying husbands on the way to the cooperative
supermarket to buy cigarettes and biscuits or
lemonade and apple pies all completely useless inputs
because the family is numbed and asleep and doped by
the giant golden logo as it lights the roads home at a
convenient crossroads to give a reward to the good
little boy or girl as payment for their performance in
the pale brick school hall where the teachers yawn
through another shallow cultural evening before
exhaling into an armchair sold like an aid to life on
interest free credit which is given by the big stores
that adorn the old marshland in front of the tinplate
works where my father used to shoot ducks before it
was built because then he lived for many years and
filled our beaks with the money he earned building
that factory where now they make tinplate and are
such an important local employer like the masters of
our town deserving a doffed cap and a place on the
magistrates bench in the grey stone building where
hopeless kids get shafted by the system because they
make the material for the dog food tins for the lonely
people whose dogs shit on my gravel in llanelli south
wales

Where is Your Song?

What is there to sing about
in the dirty valleys of Wales?
The land of my fathers' follies,
the land of Mam's poison cake.
Where sheep flood the green hills
like maggots, munching
to certain slaughter,
and pass their moronic character
to the people, through their plates.
The rivers run cold and collect
the toxic discharge that the Lords left.
The stone-walled slate-roofed mausoleums
of mediocrity, house the bigots
and the hypocrites of fear.
Why allow these demons
to inhabit our beautiful land?
Where is the sleeping Prince
who promised to return?
Wales is not a place of blood and tears.
Wales is not a deposit of dirty rain.
The evil of our history has skewered
our hearts to a red jersey,
the only paltry pride we have left.
Oh Wales, where is your song of joy?

Being Air Under Sky

From the deep, enigma
the source of the river
springing, sparkling
spreading its dream
flowing, glowing
a growing stream

Through the long, dilemma
the course of the river
shoaling, shining
shedding its blood
splashing, flashing
a dashing flood

To the wide, conundrum
the force of the river
scouring, scumbling
scuttling its breath
flaring, glaring
a sharing death

Cat

Everyone should have a cat,
if not their own a borrowed one.
The cat will sit and clean its fur,
wiggle its claws inside its ear,
stare at you from time to time,
sneer at your silly rhyme.

Early Spring Haiku

moss covering brick
last year's leaves decomposing
green appearing

February dawn
magnolia buds open
pink blossoms emerge

Moss off the roof

these pavements could use a wire brush he said
I didn't understand what he meant
the pavement was a little untidy
that's all
with a few twigs
stones
and the odd
human-created detritus
like cellophane wrappers
from cigarette packets and
chucked chewing gum
but there wasn't much
not a lot
less than you'd expect
from an inner city side-street
on a Saturday

wanting to acknowledge
the man
who passed me on the slabs
and without wanting
to look
like a fool
or make him feel
he was
I had to say something
so I said
moss off the roof
the birds have been
slinging
moss off the roof

he looked up
moss off the roof? he said
I nodded – yes I said
by now we were the length of a car apart
and still walking
but twisting our necks
as we talked
it was too much
we had to stop and face each other
moss off the roof? he said
yes I said moss off the roof
never he said
moss off the roof

I'd seen goblets of moss
dropping to the pavement
from the roof
looked up, saw a magpie
flicking
searching for grub
I suppose
I told him
it could be the birds I said
making the pavements untidy
oh he said
without understanding
moss off the roof he said
well I never

Everything Changes

The rush of existence, the crush of the game
Everything changes, it's always the same

Open the basket, dig deep inside
Gorge on potatoes, boiled, mashed, and fried

Scrub up the carrots, dice up the swede
Add in the garlic, and that's all you need

Wait for the winter, remember the snow
Laugh in the sunshine, relax in its glow

Open the window, breathe in the air
Dance when it's raining, sleep in the chair

Wind up the washing, fill up the bath
Skip in the forest, sidestep the path

Learn how to yodel, splash in the sea
Paint on a canvas, rattle a tree

Run up a mountain, pick up a flower
Think of the beauty, remember the hour

The rush of existence, the crush of the game
Everything changes, it's always the same

Gather your apples, add spice to your cake
Sing songs at midnight, spin stones on the lake

To find what is missing, open your hand
Shine lights into corners, help us understand

Keep living and giving, from here to the end
It's never so scary, when you've got a friend

Swim in the moonlight, plant seeds in the spring
Always remember, that love is the thing

Find truth in the morning, find warmth in the night
When it feels heavy, it's hiding its light

Go to the river, lie under the clouds
Hop on the pebbles, sing songs aloud

Walk along gently, see birds flying past
Look right inside you, find peace there at last

The rush of existence, the crush of the game
Everything changes, it's always the same

Forty years is a long time

forty years ago I would have called him an old man
if I had noticed him at all
he would have slippered past us in the corridor
and smelled of pee
I would have held my breath
for a step or two
and
now
he's me

I am the meat

I am the meat of my masters
their cut and come again
consumable
I am given earth and given water
I eat the sun
light
heat
and sprout for their consumption

Is it this?

Leaf: It buds, grows, absorbs, gives, falls, gives.
Wind: It blows, subsides, grows, growls, slows, blows.
Sun: It shines, sets, glows, shows.
River: It wets, carries, cuts, falls, flows.
Earth: It moves, shakes, falls, burns.
Tree: It roots, branches, barks, grows, spreads, falls.
Hill: It slopes, rises, grows, shows.

My Dragon

it is time again
it has been long coming
poking at my consciousness
in the night – asleep
or should be
but it nags

it is my dragon
I woke it
demanded its breath

it resisted
said – let me lie
I am sleeping

I said – you are a dragon
not a dog

it sighed
and complied

now it nags
when neglected

yaps, bites
sometimes snarls

I sigh
and try
to comply

Cambridge

I wonder if –

This bridge over
the river Cam
Was ever?

It's a nice location
a good flow
and there must have been
Popes here once.

Now there are bats
and swans
and polite dossers
drinking from cans
that later
float.

You can eat rice
wrapped in seaweed
and curries galore

Swans duck
dip for food
Ducks swan
(They can be a bit rude)

Cab drivers from Croatia
posh nobs from Asia
eating chips
Avocado dips
Batters at crease
on Parker's Piece

The cost of everything
should be measured
by cubic metres of sewage
it's a good indication
of activity

resource – usage

Polite alcoholics
pass the time
on Petersfield
until the night shelter opens
drinking from cans
and sometimes sleeping
in the sun

Babble

Here it rolls
despite the babble
people babble
people trouble
Babbling
People
Babbling People
Trouble

Trouble-babble-people
People
with their ths and
ychs and isses and
rrrs and ccs
They stick their
yuckiness
in all my ears
They clog my breath
and hurt me
with their words
Hard words
dropping
like
tiles from a roof
and hurting
with their hardness

But that's what
poems are for
To put words in
their place
Show them who's boss
Bounce them together
Tie them in
unwanted matrimony
like soft-satin-ballpoint
black ink on white sheet
rock hard mistakes

Jackdaws in CAR PARKS

Jackdaws
in CAR PARKS
where they shouldn't be

But then
ppl
eat cheap tarts
and drop crumbs
everywhere
I wouldn't like to be a jackdaw
Being a bit of a fussy eater

FOR INSTANCE

I wouldn't eat a slowworm
even if I was starving

BUT JACKDAWS
eat almost everything

They have no lines in their minds
except that possibly
(and I don't know this for sure)
They won't eat their own eggs

I suppose if they did
they wouldn't exist

Imagine that you're the last jackdaw
in the world
and the only thing left to eat
is your one remaining egg
which is about to hatch

do you gobble it up
even though you know
that however long you live
afterwards

There'll never be another jackdaw
or maybe you could

MATE with a sparrow

and have babies
called
Jackrow or Spardaw

What if you lay on top of your egg
and quietly died
Your decomposition
feeding your young

Then it'd grow up
and have a different dilemma
but at least it'd have

A LIFE

What comes last?
The jackdaw – or
THE EGG

Cwl Cymru

Now, there is a small spring of clear water
whispering in the hills.
There is a homeopathic gleam
in the still-black rain still.

For the Welsh are a wise people
and have kept their secrets,
under the century-old slag-heap
where a diamond hid its facets.

Now, we are assembled in Cardiff,
we shine in London and the States.
We chew the cud with movie stars,
share the glitter with our mates.

We'll play in front of thousands,
blow horns on prime-time shows.
We'll show the world what we can do
as our re-found kudos grows.

We're more than just an oval ball
black dust, green grass and sheep.
It's time to sing our song again
the Prince has roused from sleep.

Finding a Voice.

They say find your voice,
these esteemed poets.
So I tried.
I looked on top of the linepost
and there it was,
so I thought.
I crawled under the shed
and the worms cried
so I heard.
I wandered into the kitchen,
turned the tap on,
so I drank.
I looked in the attic, the bedroom, the garden
and the outside loo.
I looked in my shoe.
Then I looked in the mirror
and opened my mouth,
and there it was,
I'd swallowed it.

Christmas Day

This time of year, there are loads of things
things to think about
people
places
events
things
lots of things
things that glitter
things that sparkle
(sometimes metaphorically)
reds
greens
whites
(white at least)
is white the only pure colour?
or does even that need a touch of blue
to shine?

In a Shell

Myself is in a shell,
Being hung up
And that.
I shed my shell,
From now
And then.
I am being sat,
Upon a wave of Freeness.
My shell is shed,
But what
Do I find to be done.
In the phase,
It's hot
Outside it's muchly warm.
I am being moved myself,
But be looked
Onto scorn.

We Us-self do change
Our scenes and our shells
And in the interim of truth
We've such a much to tell.

Glastonbury '98

where has it gone?
has it gone?
was it ever there?
was it ever?
or in my imagination?
the green barbarous fields
ripping the soles
barring the way
a divine consciousness shared
and left alone
in a wide green field
where the cows usually shit
and the grown-up children
roll in the mud
thinking it's cool
and in-touch
but we now know
that illusion
of those times in our young days
in the blitz
or the warehouse
or the hedge
or the army
or a shared house in manchester
or especially in college
where we all were
at oxford and cambridge
especially in london
where the people sit
in shiny metal cans

and reach for the stars
by looking at their feet
with dear daps
slip slop along the concrete arteries
to work
and earn
so that they can sleep on the damp green grass
and smoke the dry brownish stuff
so now
moving back
in body
to almost certain disappointment
to find the egg of enlightenment
fried on a bun
with a neatly round slice of bacon
from a pig's back
on your head
you continue to choose
the easy life
of taste and feeling
ingesting a thousand screams
on toast
for breakfast
mastitis on toast for lunch
bovine growth hormone soup for supper
served with a slice of horse

Lifers Left

Thursday morning in Llanelli.

Many are nodding acquaintances.
 Lots of Welsh,
   Ageing sisters,
       The old,
           The infirm,
            The jobless
                   No-hopers.
        TRAPPED.
The nowhere-to-goers,
        Lifeless in Cheap Cafes,
      Faces washed out like their hair.

A team of cold-fingered witless window cleaners:
        "you do this side".
       They're attacking the street.
       Squee(je)ing a few coppers.
The only hope for the human race,
   a gang of construction workers,
   imported from
      out-of-town,
    with a charming
       slyness,
         a wily life,
   a gleam,
     a challenging look.
   They're from OUTSIDE,
      just visiting,
       not yet drained of blood.

ppl

ppl
streaming
thru car parks
carrying bags

Perusing shelves of junk
commodities
consumables
comestibles   (whatever that means. I
                heard Reg Holdsworth
                say it once on
                Coronation Street -
                something to do
                with supermarkets)

Here – the supermarkets
are full
of CRAP

and ppl
STREAM
thru Car Parks
with fat arses
and glasses
more often than not

Gammy legs and grandchildren
Granny drives
Grandpa wants to assert
his authority
trying his best to look hard
even though – he's not allowed to drive
any more

Weekend

There are bacon sandwiches
and then there are:
mountains of dying lambs
– organic compost
made from blood;
Traditional Sundays
– walks by the river
flush with red.

There is green jelly
and then there is:
an ocean of putrid blubber
– blooming algae
made from stench;
a useful Saturday
– a trip to shop
cursed by cash.

Liars

Drunken mothers tell lies
not mine, not mine
Drunken mothers tell lies
about their children
about their children
My wife
the mother of my child
drunken mothers tell lies
about their children
about their children
not mine, not mine
except perhaps on her sixtieth birthday
when she got drunk
but not too drunk
because my father was dying
from a stroke and cancer
but he came
but he came
before he knew about the cancer
drunken mothers tell lies
about their children
about their children.

Fart

I stood on a bridge
nothing more than a silhouette
to those chargers of the headlight brigade.
One vehicle – a slow-moving camper van
stopped under the bridge,
and in the pauses between stampedes
I heard a fart
I laughed then
I don't know why
I always laugh at farts
(but not fart jokes
or joking farts)
They're so funny.

Stupid Things

Stupid things are edible
Glenda told me so.
Have you ever seen
the dumb look in a sheep's eyes?
And cows, sure they're appealing
in a doey sort of way.
But come on?
Intelligent?
I don't think so.
Now dogs are different,
they're clever, loyal, bright.
I love the little buggers
buggers, buggers.
Yes dogs are different,
except,
except,
except in Korea.

Happy New You

Then – the day – the darkest day and the day filled
with the most light and the most abandon – no buses
to catch or cars to drive, no limits, no mercy to your
lives.
Loved ones come and go, bins overflow. 'Thank God it's
all over.'
All over.
All over.
Crisp New Year
except it's not
it's wet and not cold enough
and the places you've been
stay with you
and make you cough and moan
Get a grip on yourself
Get a grip
So you do
and you notice
the nights lightening
the days' cool sun returning
– reviving.
And you return
You are you again
but you are a different you
an evolved through pain
and darkness you
A new you
A happy new you

Eat me, Keep me

Bananas, they say,
are the best selling item
Packets of sweet mush
With a banana flavour

A bit like the girl
I dreamt of last night
Except she had dark hair
But still tasted like a banana

Every banana comes to an end
its yellow skin blackening
and the trick is
to catch it while it's ripe
and ready
to eat.

Twin Towers

I was wounded first –
the blow caught me in the neck.
I couldn't breathe,
Then –
with a whoosh of fire,
my mouth opened
and huge clouds of smoke fled out.
I didn't realise I had such energy,
such love.
I smiled when I knew I was dying;
I always said I would go first.
You watched as I choked, incredulously,
not wanting to believe
in my mortality.
My belly shook, I retched and coughed,
but your strength,
the power of your gaze,
began to mend.
Then –
you were smacked in the chest;
a direct hit to your heart,
and you shuddered
but you didn't scream;
there was no sound
yet.
That's when I caught your eye;
that's when I knew
we were both going to die.
In that silent lightless time
I watched, still wounded,
still breathing burning breath,

Then –
you deflated with a groan
that shook the world.
I stood, shocked, alone in emptiness
that spread like nothing
through the universe.
With no light left, I crumbled too;
we sighed together, merged –
forever
in mounds of dirt.
Then –
I knew that love can never die
not even then, not in that place
where the world was witness
to our hurt.

The End of the World

On July the twenty-fourth
nineteen-ninety-nine,
the world will end.
If not then,
then certainly in the year two-thousand,
when the New Age dawns.
All from all time will have to account
for their behaviour, and will be judged
according to their ability.
So only the dull will enter,
the gates of the Abattoir,
and become Angel fodder.
Time and Space, here and then
will be gone as if,
as if,
they were only
ripples on the divine mind.
But for George and Tim,
and Mary and Louise,
the World ended in 1998,
when they died,
from cars or cancer.
It's no big deal,
the end of the World,
just another statistic,
but no-one there,
to record it.

.